Drumset Syncopation

ADVANCED TECHNIQUES AND STUDIES FOR PLAYING BETWEEN THE BEATS

BY BRUCE R. PATZER

ISBN 978-1-4768-1384-4

HAL•LEONARD®
CORPORATION

7777 W. BLUEMOUND RD. P.O. BOX 13819 MILWAUKEE, WI 53213

In Australia Contact:
Hal Leonard Australia Pty. Ltd.
4 Lentara Court
Cheltenham, Victoria, 3192 Australia
Email: ausadmin@halleonard.com.au

Visit Hal Leonard Online at
www.halleonard.com

preface

Just as a rest is as equally effective as a note in music, a note played between the beat can be used for increased emphasis. It is this element of rhythm–of playing between the beat (pulse)–that *The Syncopated Drumset* seeks to develop.

It's hard to find an instrument that doesn't use syncopation to one degree or another; maybe a bass drum that plays on all four beats in a march. Usually, syncopation is a natural part of our past and an integral part of our future. There are two instruments that, arguably, are the most demanding when it comes to syncopation: piano and drumset.

It is not my intent for this method book to be a study on all four limbs working independently from each other. Rather, I seek to teach a new way of looking at syncopation and how it can be used in today's music. I hope you have as much fun playing through this book as I did writing it.

about the author

Bruce R. Patzer received his bachelor's degree in Percussion and Music Education from the Oberlin Conservatory of Music in Oberlin, Ohio. He obtained his master's degree from Northern Illinois University in Dekalb, Illinois. He has held the position of Band Director in three different public school systems.

Bruce has played extensively with groups in the styles of rock, funk, jazz, and blues. He has also written and arranged songs for the bands he has played with. Bruce teaches private lessons, primarily on drumset, in his home studio in the Chicago area.

acknowledgments

First, I'd like to thank my dear wife, Cyndee, who showed great patience during this project and shared in my excitement when something new was discovered. Next I would like to acknowledge my parents, who were there every step of the way to encourage me with my music and allow me the freedom to follow my chosen path. I would be remiss in not mentioning the teachers and mentors that went before me: Paul Peebles, David Peebles, Mike Stiers, and Mr. Willey, all from the public schools. From college, I'd like to thank all the music faculty from Knox College and my private instructor Mike Rosen from the Oberlin Conservatory of Music. I'd also like to recognize Larry Rossi as a local leader in music education, whom I also think of as one of my mentors. To write a drumset method book such as this is not an abstract exercise in creating notation. Rather, it is a recreation of some of the material I have used in my forty years of drumming with the countless groups in which I have played. I hope working from this book will be both a learning and creative experience for you.

contents

warm-ups for Hands and Feet

In the following warm-ups, the hands, wrists, and fingers should stay loose, never tense. The first exercise should be played at the same speed, regardless of the number of strokes played per hand. Do two warm-ups every time you practice.

DRUM KEY

syncopation

Many rhythms have combinations of notes played on the beat and off the beat. Here is an example where the emphasis is on the beat.

If a rhythm has important, emphasized notes that are played off the beat, that rhythm is said to be syncopated. An example is the bossa-nova clave, which has emphasized notes on the "and" of 2 in the first bar and the "and" of 3 in the second bar.

In the following example, the sixteenth notes on the "a" of 2 and the "e" of 3 in the snare drum and the "a" of 3 in the bass drum give the beat a syncopated feel.

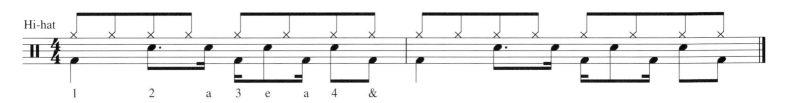

Even though the next example has snare drum notes on the "and" of 2 and 4, the overall beat does not feel syncopated due to the strong pulse on the four main beats.

EXPANDING SNARE DRUM AND BASS DRUM RHYTHMS

Utilizing the bass drum

Adding the hi-hat with the left foot

On the example below, the snare accents are on the beat.

Drum break from "Satisfaction" by the Rolling Stones with snare accents on the beat

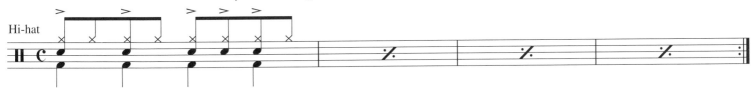

This example uses the high tom.

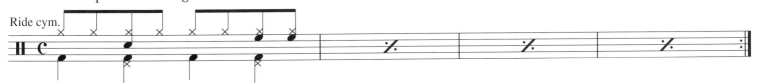

Bass drum playing in between the beat

Accents (>) and counts 2 and 4 are played louder. The other notes are syncopated (played in between the beat) and usually played softer. They are sometimes called ghost notes.

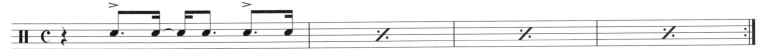

Expanding snare drum and bass drum rhythms

On snare, accent 2 and 4. The other notes are syncopated and usually played softer (as ghost notes).

BASIC ROCK

Quarter notes on the downbeat

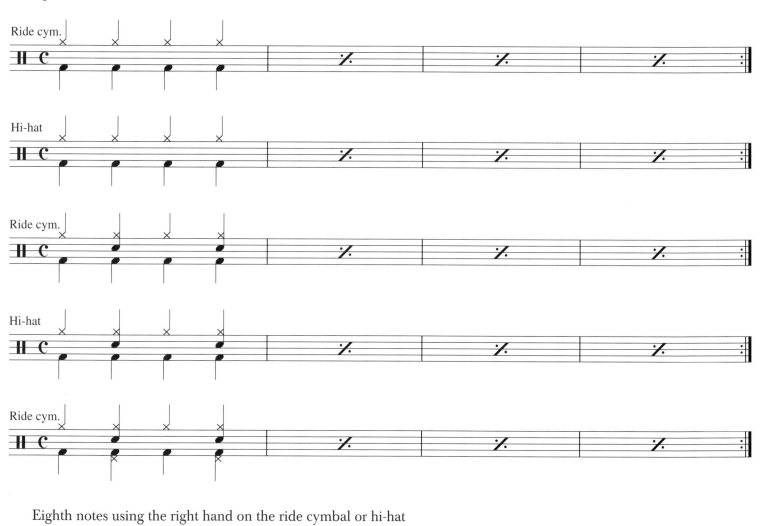

Eighth notes using the right hand on the ride cymbal or hi-hat

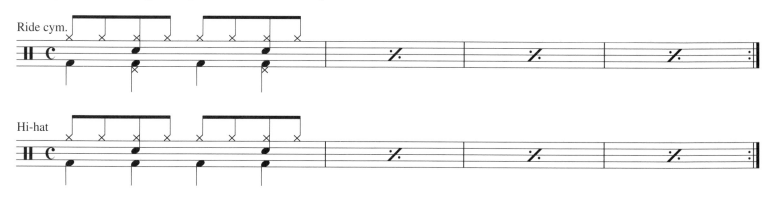

Using the left hand on the snare to create more variations

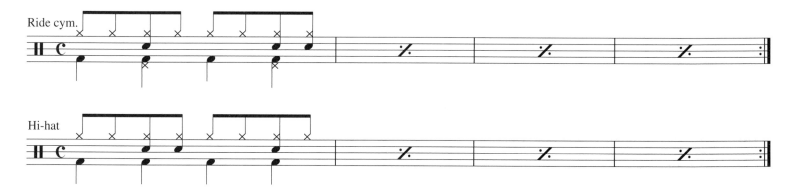

USING BASS DRUM TO CREATE BASIC ROCK PATTERNS

1st time hi-hat; 2nd time ride cymbal

USING SNARE DRUM AND BASS DRUM TO CREATE
SYNCOPATED BEATS

ONE-BAR FILLS OFF THE HI-HAT

Usually, a short break or solo is called a fill. It connects two or more sections of a piece. Play the bass drum and crash at the end of the fill on count 1 of the repeat. In the first three measures of each example, play a beat of your choice from page 10.

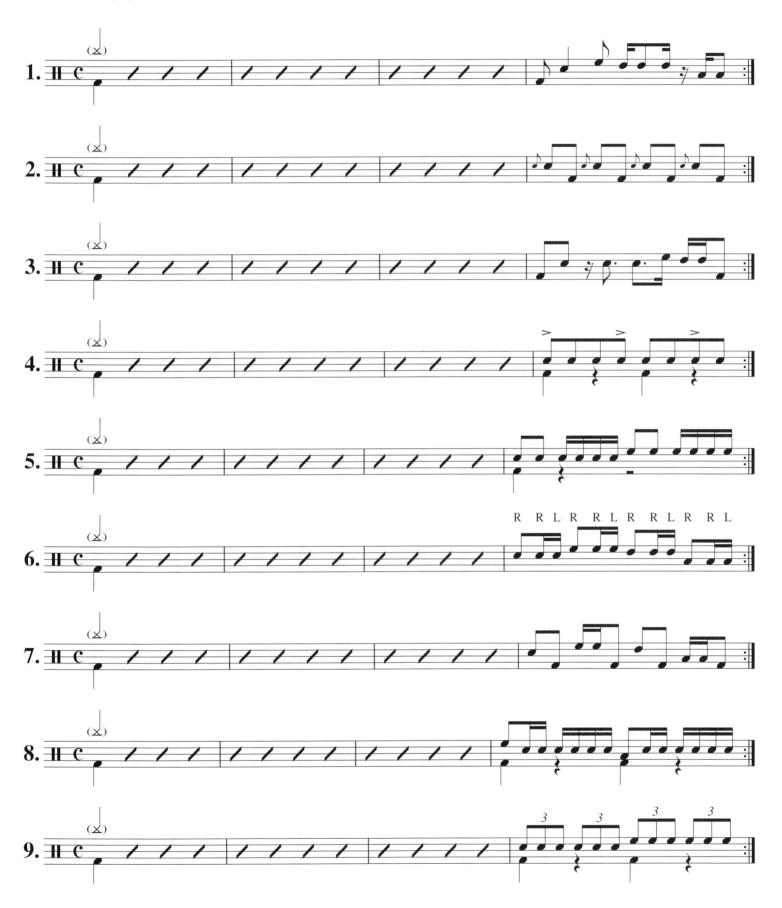

TWO-BAR FILLS OFF THE RIDE CYMBAL

Play the bass drum and crash at the end of the fill on count 1 of the repeat. In the first two measures of each example, play a beat of your choice from page 10.

FOUR-BAR SOLOS

Play a beat for four measures and then play one of the four-bar solos below. Begin each solo with a cymbal crash, and play a cymbal crash on beat 1 when returning to the beat after the solo.

The main beats (rhythms) used in this book

Funk Rock: Eighth Notes

Soul: Eighth Note on Ride Cymbal

Two-Hand Hi-Hat Beats

Bell of Ride Cymbal After Beats with Right Hand

Driving Beat

Latin Beats

Bossa Nova with Rim Click

Reggae

Slow Blues

Shuffle

Jazz

Country

FUNK-ROCK BEATS

Play the following beats the first time through using the hi-hat. On the repeat, play the beat using the ride cymbal and using the left foot to play the hi-hat on counts 2 and 4.

ONE-BAR FILLS

Sometimes "fills" can be played without using the toms. Playing a variation on a beat can create the rhythmic intensity and excitement of a regular fill, yet it has the advantage of never breaking the flow of the beat. For these two pages, you should use a variety of beats from pages 15 and 16. Play time for three measures, and play the fill on the fourth measure. I have used beat 4 from page 15 as an example on this page, and beat 11 from page 16 as an example on page 18.

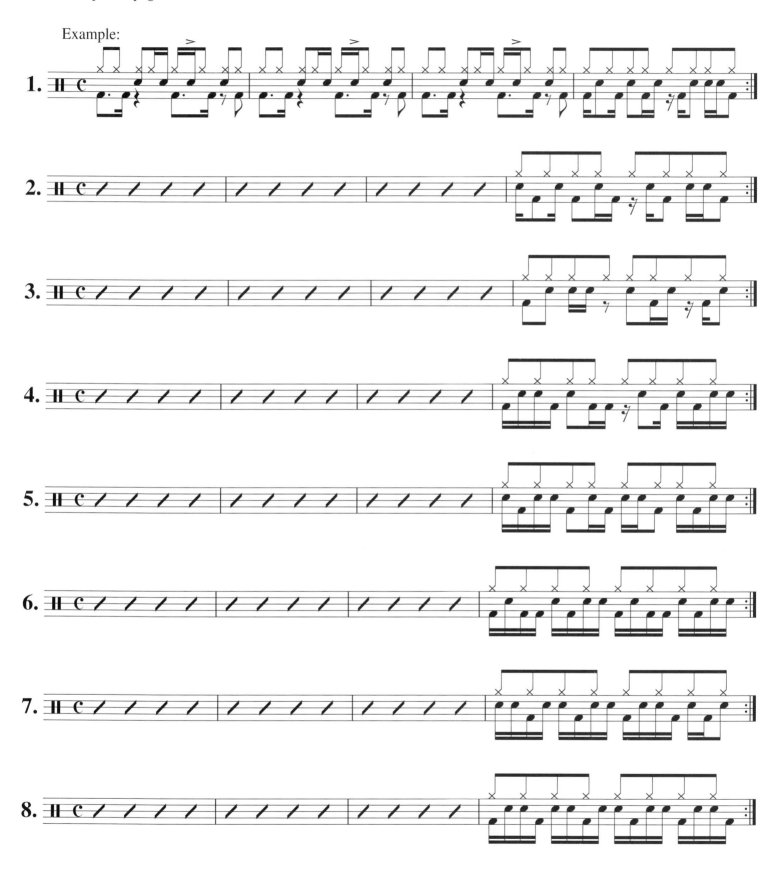

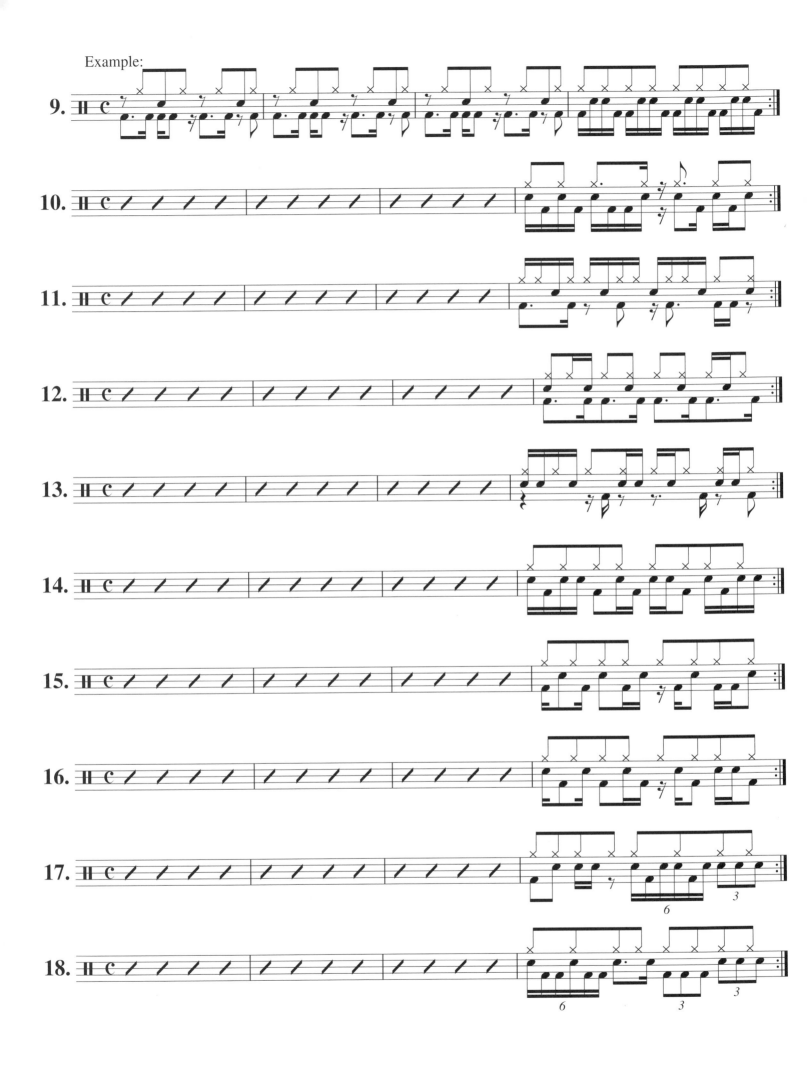

FILLS WITH TOMS

Here are some more conventional fills where both hands are freed up from playing time. Always play three bars of time before playing the fill. Choose your beats from pages 15 and 16 as well as using some of the rhythmic fills from pages 17 and 18, doubling them as a beat. Remember to play the exercise the first time through using the hi-hat. On the repeat, play the right hand on the ride cymbal, using the left foot to play counts 2 and 4 on the hi-hat. The fills should end with a crash and a bass drum on count 1 of the first bar of the repeat. I have used fill 14 from page 18 as an example.

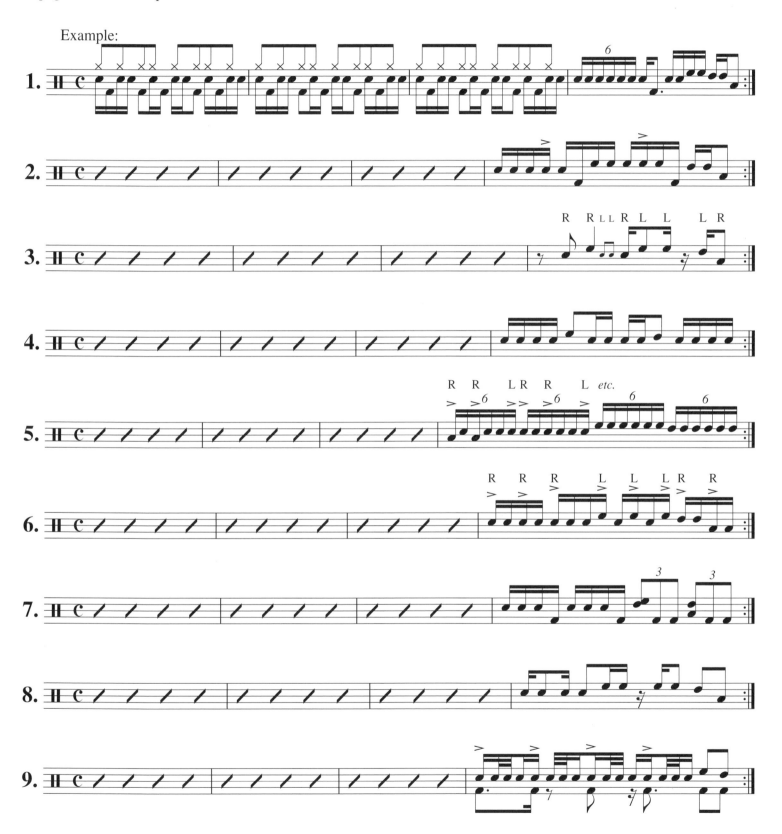

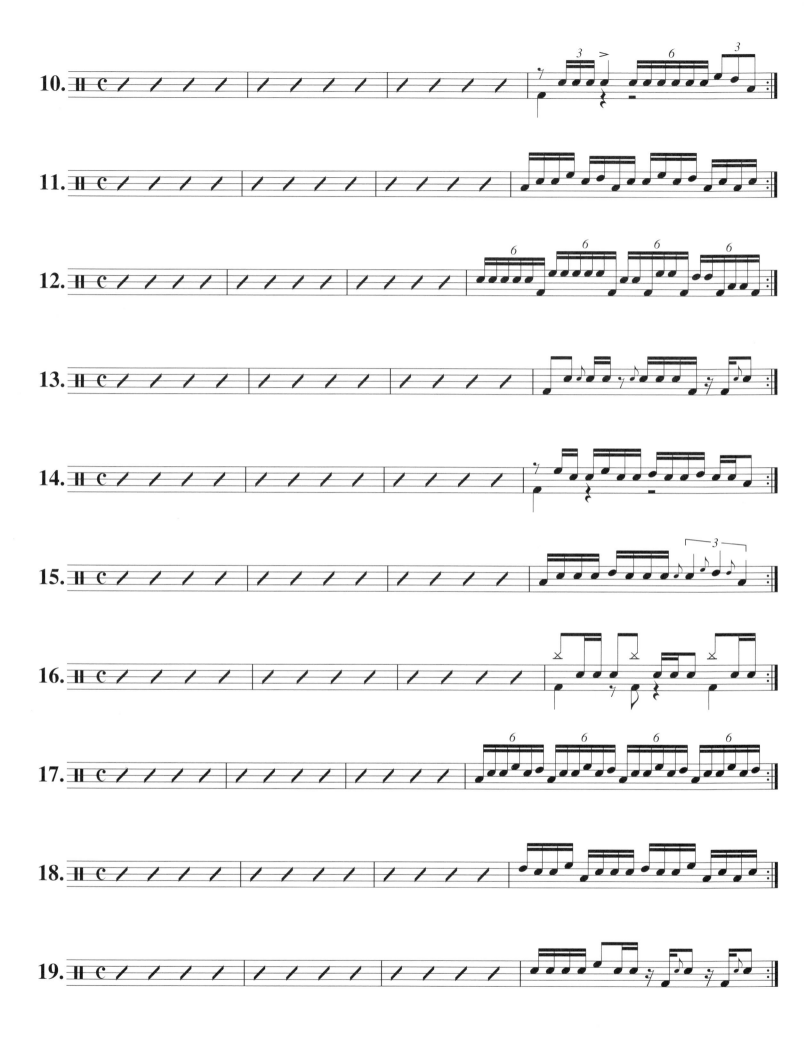

TWO-HAND HI-HAT BEATS

"MESSIN' WITH THE KID"

This is a Motown-style (Detroit soul) piece. The ghost notes on the snare give it that funky feel.

"WITHOUT LOVE"

As recorded by the Doobie Brothers

latin beats

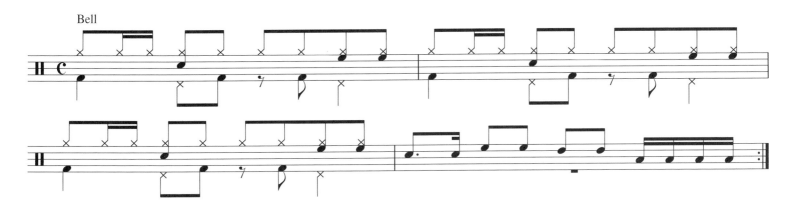

BOSSA NOVA WITH RIM CLICKS

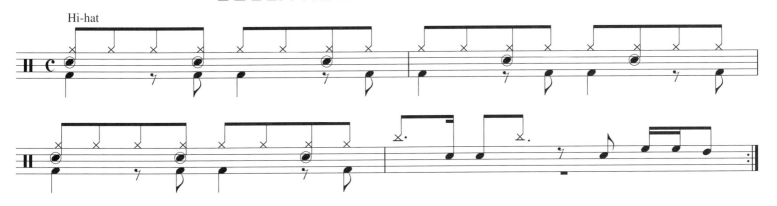

BOSSA NOVA ON BASS DRUM

SAMBA WITH FILLS

REGGAE

Play with the right hand on the afterbeat.

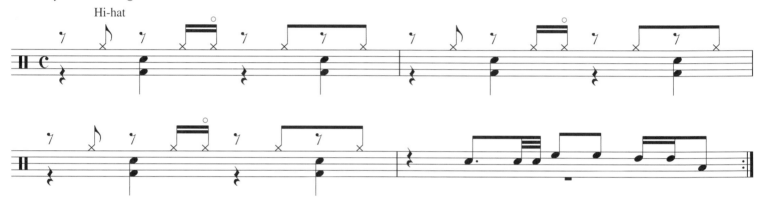

REGGAE WITH A BOUNCE

slow blues

As before, the first time through, use the hi-hat, and the second time through use the ride cymbal, using the left foot on the hi-hat pedal to play counts 2 and 4.

BLUES FILLS

Choose a variety of beats from pages 27–28 and, without using the toms, play three measures of time before playing the fill. End the fill with a crash on 1 on the first note on the repeat.

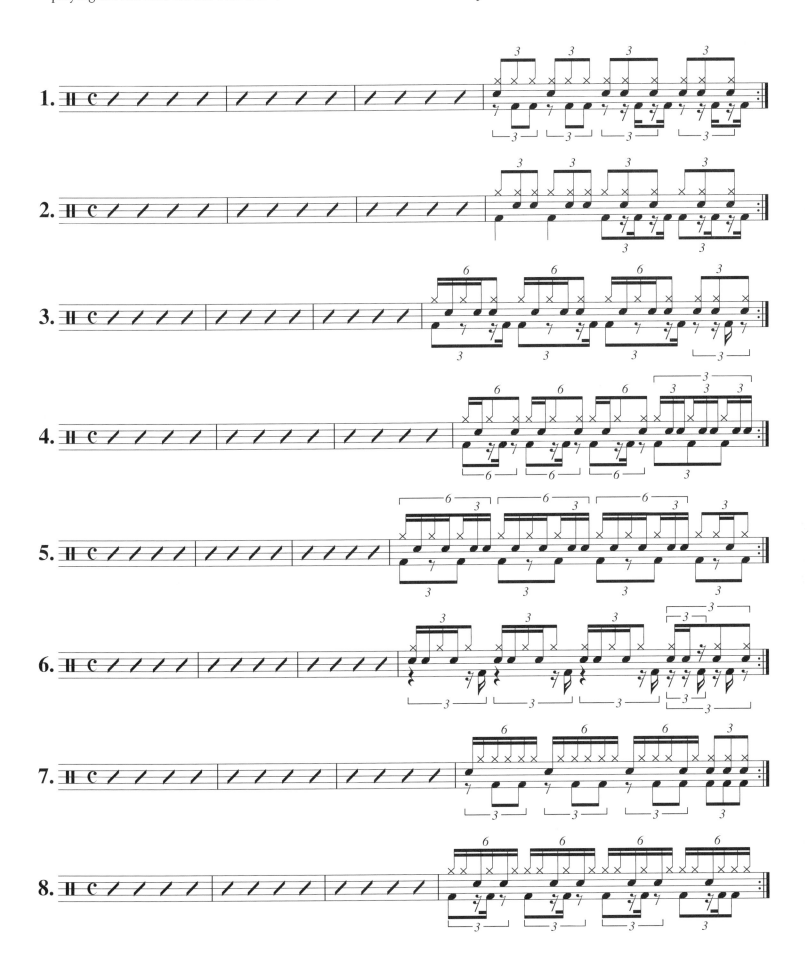

BLUES FILLS WITH TOMS

These fills are typically played on the last measure of a 12-bar blues.

shuffle beats

If you look at page 37, you can see that the jazz beat and shuffle are closely related. Play the following shuffles on the ride cymbal, using the left foot to play the hi-hat on 2 and 4.

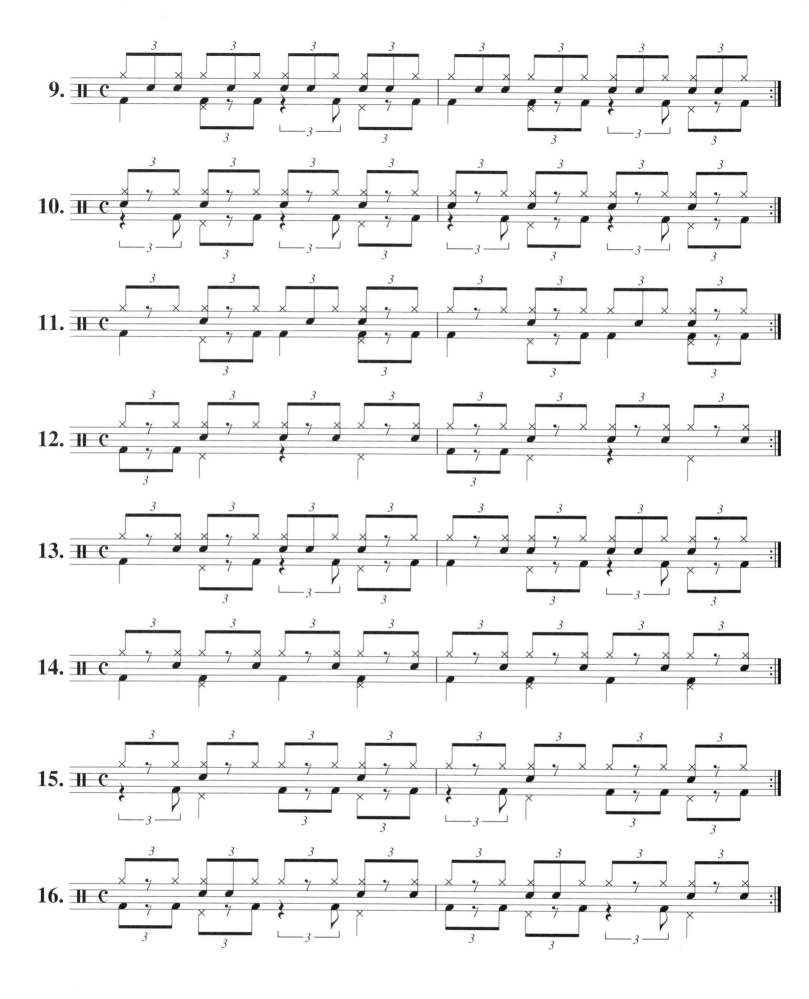

ONE-BAR FILLS

Play three bars of time by choosing any shuffle beats from pages 31–32. Do the fill on the fourth measure, ending with a crash on count 1.

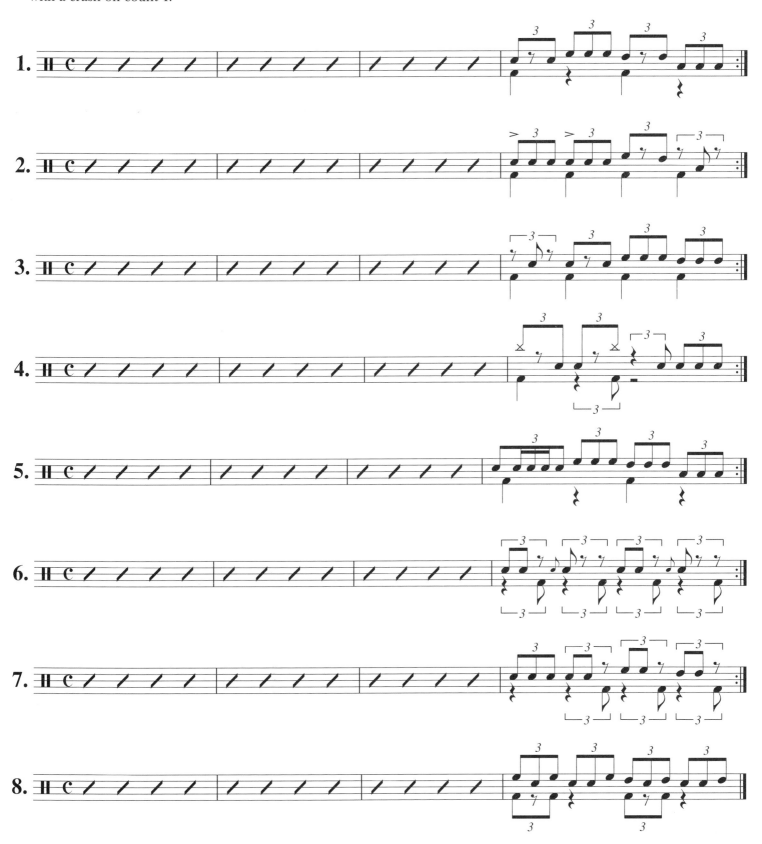

TWO-BAR FILLS

The two bars of time should consist of a variety of beats from pages 31–32. The two-bar fills should end with a crash on beat 1.

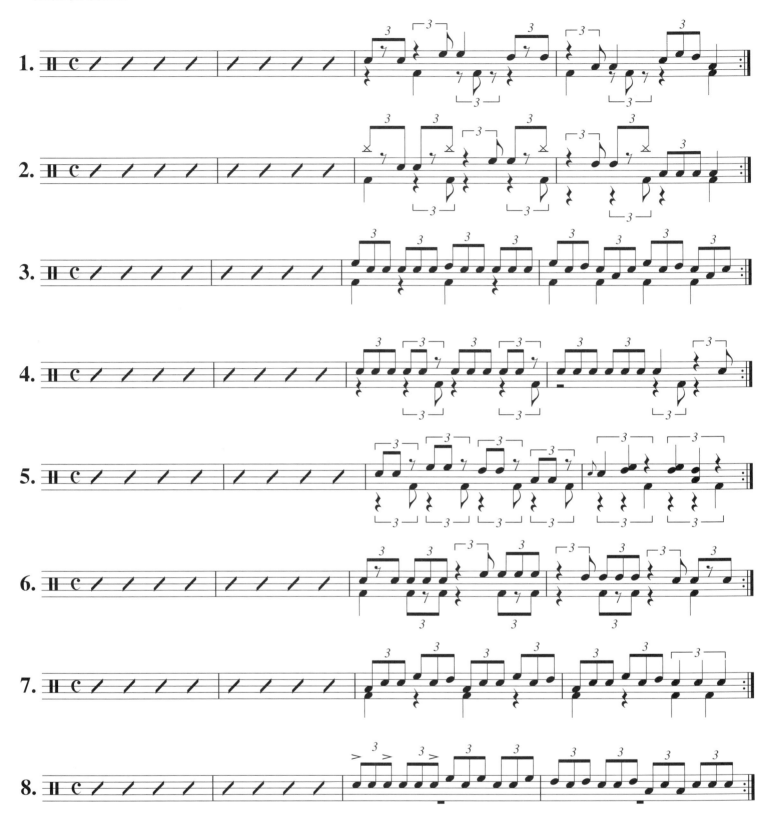

country/gospel

The following exercises include beats and fills.

Upbeat

Medium tempo

Laid back

JAZZ

CYMBAL-SNARE COMBINATIONS

CYMBAL-BASS DRUM COMBINATIONS

SNARE-BASS DRUM COMBINATIONS

FOUR-WAY COMBINATIONS

JAZZ RHYTHMS

TWO-BAR JAZZ FILLS

Play two bars of time using the jazz beats from pages 41 and 42 before playing the fill.

JAZZ DRUM CHARTS

As Written

As Played

46

JAZZ IN 3 AND 5

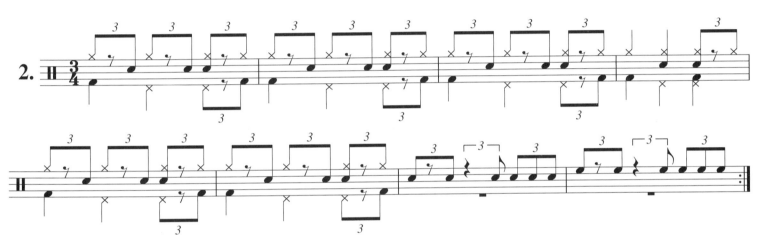

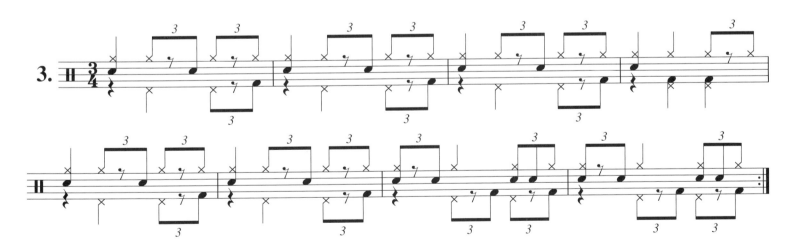

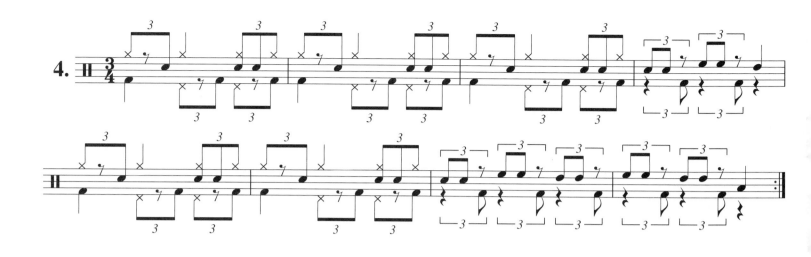